Arizona
on my mind

" *Arizona is away off at the end of the world,"*
exclaims an eastern paper. Yep! Away off at the end
of the world, next door to heaven. "

Yuma Daily Examiner, 1908

The
Globe
Pequot
Press

Guilford, Connecticut

Early morning light casting rosy hues over the Grand Canyon from Yavapai Point   ERIC WUNROW

" To see the Grand Canyon full of purple smoke at dawn or sublimely fired at sunset, is to be elevated in soul. To see the red rocks; the alkali flats like snow; the sand dunes so graceful and curved; the long cedar slopes, speckled green and gray, leading up to the bold peaks; the vast black belts of timber; the Navajo facing the sunrise with his silent prayer, the Hopi in his alfalfa fields, or the Apache along the historical Apache Trail; the coyote sneaking through the arroyos; the lonely cliff dwellings with their monuments of a vanished race; the endless slopes of sage, green and gray and purple on the heights; the natural stone bridges and the petrified forests—and a thousand more beautiful sights—that is to see Arizona. "

Zane Grey,
"An Appreciation of the Grand Canyon"

Sandpaper mule's ears blooming in the shadows of the Coyote Buttes, in Paria Canyon-Vermilion Cliffs Wilderness   LARRY ULRICH

Autumn aspens create a golden pathway at Hart Prairie in the San Francisco Peaks LARRY ULRICH

Visions of the tropics in the Grand Canyon: Venus maidenhair ferns and clear cascades on Royal Arch Creek   LARRY ULRICH

Morning stillness on the Colorado River flowing through Imperial National Wildlife Refuge   RANDY A. PRENTICE

Great egret   DONALD M. JONES

Water, earth, and sky combine and contrast at Glen Canyon National Recreation Area   JEFF FOOTT

Reflections of the towering spires of Cathedral the Crescent Moon Recreation Area near Sedona   KERRICK JAMES

An Arizona icon, the saguaro cactus thrives in Arizona's unique climate, like this hillside in the Tonto National Monument outside Phoenix
TERRY DONNELLY

> "*Driving through a saguaro forest for the first time makes you a little self-conscious. You get the odd feeling of walking into a crowded room, where everybody stops what he was doing and watches in embarrassed silence till you have passed through.*"

Reg Manning,
What Kinda Cactus Izzat?

Spring beauty: a saguaro cactus blooming at its namesake monument in the Sonoran desert JEFF FOOTT

The snow-capped San Francisco Peaks provide a backdrop to the Lomaki ruins in the Wupatki National Monument   LAURENCE PARENT

Constructed entirely from blocks of local Moenkopi sandstone, the Wukoki, or "big house" pueblo, built by the Sinagua Indians more than 600 years ago   TOM DANIELSEN

The massive Casa Grande dominates the ruins of a prehistoric Hohokam agricultural village at Casa Grande Ruins National Monument
TOM DANIELSEN

Agate house and pottery shards, the leavings of an ancient civilization, Petrified Forest National Park
RUSS FINLEY/BORLAND STOCK PHOTO

The white dome of the church at Tumacacori National Historical Park with the Santa Rita Mountains in the background JACK W. DYKINGA

The stark, white walls and straight lines of Mission San Xavier del Bac contrast with the rough landscape and pastel sky   RANDY A. PRENTICE

Inside the mission   RANDALL K. ROBERTS

❝ If Arizona has one building more notable than any other, one link with the first advent of the white man into this region, it must be Mission San Xavier del Bac . . . . It is a place of great color, and dazzling brilliance. Here there is much joy and laughter, and it is a fine place to be for even a few moments. ❞

Carlos H. Elmer,
Arizona in Color

A medicine wheel near Sedona CHEYENNE ROUSE

Supai Indian children enjoying a ride ERIC WUNROW

"Desert varnish" stains the sandstone cliffs above the White House ruins in Canyon de Chelly National Monument   KERRICK JAMES

Brittlebush and a few lonely saguaros lead the way to the Superstition Mountains in the Tonto National Forest   TOM TILL

A leaning yucca framing distant Baboquivari Peak at Buenos Aires National Wildlife Refuge   JACK W. DYKINGA

A pair of Gambel's quail   JEFF FOOTT

" Arizona! A magic word. Arizona! What visions of grandeur those seven letters conjure. Arizona! A symphony in mad, extravagant colors, shaded with the soft light of the desert in the evening, the purple mountains at twilight, the mauve sky of a rising sun. . . . To all men and all women there is a different Arizona. But to all men as to all women there is one overwhelming Arizona—that is Arizona, the land of great beauty, and Arizona, the land of rich, magnificent color. Arizona! "

Raymond Carlson,
Arizona's Scenic Seasons

The natural water slide at Slide Rock State Park, one of the best places to beat the heat on a July afternoon RANDY A. PRENTICE

Hikers reveling in the power and spirit of nature at Mooney Falls in the Grand Canyon   JAMES RANDKLEV

Hanging on tight on a raft trip through the muddy waters of the Colorado River   DAVID BENNER/F-STOCK INC.

“We have an unknown distance yet to run, an unknown river to explore. What falls there are, we know not; what rocks beset the channel, we know not; what walls rise over the river, we know not. Ah, well! we may conjecture many things.”

John Wesley Powell,
The Exploration of the Colorado River and Its Canyons

Happy mud bather on the Little Colorado River   CHARLIE BORLAND/BORLAND STOCK PHOTO

Navigating the steep canyon walls and blue-green waters of Havasu Creek   GLEN ALLISON/F-STOCK INC.

Prime campsite: a lone houseboat occupies the waters below Gunsight Butte in Lake Powell's Glen Canyon National Recreation Area
TOM TILL

186-mile-long Lake Powell, with its many canyons, coves, and fingers, has more shoreline than the coast of California   ERIC WUNROW

Glen Canyon Dam holds back the Colorado River to form Lake Powell   RANDALL K. ROBERTS

"O yes, I have heard of that country—it is just like hell. All it lacks is water and good society."

An Ohio senator during
congressional discussion of
territorial status for Arizona, 1862

A climber clinging to a sheer rock wall at Windy Point in the Santa Catalina Mountains PETER NOEBELS

Penthouse view and first-class accommodations in the Painted Desert   ERIC WUNROW

❝ There's something about the desert that doesn't like man, something that mocks his nesting instinct and makes his constructions look feeble and temporary. Yet it's just that inhospitableness that endears the arid rockiness, the places pointy and poisonous, to men looking for its discipline.❞

William Least Heat Moon,
Blue Highways

Dog tired after a day's hike on the Supai Trail   ERIC WUNROW

The aqua-blue waters of the Little Colorado River are a popular stopover for whitewater rafters   CHARLIE BORLAND/F-STOCK INC.

Splashing down: a different kind of whitewater in Tempe   KERRICK JAMES

Luxury houseboats and tourboats cruising Lake Powell   BUDDY MAYS/TRAVEL STOCK

Jet skiers zooming along in the last light of the day   FRANK OBERLE

Rain clouds and a setting sun combine to paint this fiery sky above Sabino Canyon in the Santa Catalina Mountains   DAVID W. LAZAROFF

Rocky Mountain maples adorn the North Rim of the Grand Canyon in fall colors   LES MANEVITZ

Light rules here with indescribable brightness. The clear air conspires with light, so that distant horizons are magnified; peaks a hundred miles away appear near at hand. Nor does the conspiracy cease at sunset. Desert mountains and thunderheads reach for the retreating light, and give it back to earth as gilded afterglow.

Rowe Findley,
Great American Deserts

Northern cardinal   C. ALLAN MORGAN

Golden aspens carpet the ground below the San Francisco Peaks, Arizona's highest mountains, in the Coconino National Forest
RANDY A. PRENTICE

Reflections of an Arizona autumn in Sabino Creek, Santa Catalina Mountains   DAVID W. LAZAROFF

Golden fire created by autumn aspens and fading light at the edge of the Hart Prairie Nature Conservancy Preserve   JACK W. DYKINGA

❝ Arizona is famous for her beautiful deserts, the haven of winter visitors. . . .
But there is another Arizona beyond the deserts that many casual travelers often
fail to see—the forests. Arizona's vast forest lands are a rich natural asset. ❞

Joseph Garrison Pearce,
"Arizona's First Forest Ranger" in
Arizona Memories

Somewhere between fall and winter: leaves on the trees, snow on the ground, leaves on the snow   TOM DANIELSEN

An early spring snowstorm leaves a frosting on Sunset Crater northeast of Flagstaff   TOM DANIELSEN

Accented by snow and sun, the buttes of Monument Valley Navajo Tribal Park present an inspiring image   TOM TILL

A hardy pinyon clinging precariously to the rim of the Grand Canyon while storm clouds threaten   TOM DANIELSEN

A winter afternoon in Coal Canyon on the Navajo Reservation   TOM DANIELSEN

Descending the rocky summit of Mount Wrightson in the
Santa Rita Mountains   JACK W. DYKINGA

*" When you live in a big land, but not
over-populated, just a few minutes drive
and there you are; in the tranquil world of
Nature. . . . Here the boundary of one's
world is the shimmering horizon even
beyond where the mountains are nothing
more than hazy, purple curtains. Our
world has no boundaries. Our thoughts
and dreams and hopes soar beyond the
boundaries of our world and, perhaps,
that is the very essence of tranquillity. "*

Raymond Carlson,
Arizona's Scenic Seasons

Offices of Tombstone's historic newspaper, the *Epitaph*, established in 1880   TOM TILL

Scene of the Old West's most famous gunfight, the O.K. Corral in Tombstone
RANDALL K. ROBERTS

Sunshine girls and shady characters in Old Tucson   FRANK OBERLE

Popular watering hole in Tombstone   RANDALL K. ROBERTS

" *Here lies Lester Moore*
Shot with a .44
No Les, No more "

Tombstone epitaph at Boot Hill Graveyard

Kitsch on Route 66: Snow Cap Burgers in Seligman   KERRICK JAMES

" The world is fed up with today: people are looking for yesterday, they are looking for the simpler times, and naturally they want to travel the highway that touched practically anyone and any family that you speak to. "

Angel Delgaldillo,
Historic Route 66 Association

Nostalgia along one of America's most famous byways   TOM BROWNOLD

The Longhorn Building in Amado LAURENCE PARENT

Burros still cruise Main Street in Oatman MARK E. GIBSON

Unique southwestern art market in Jerome   MARK E. GIBSON

"The arts in Arizona are and always will be unique because they are driven by engines that are uniquely our own; our history, which still lies close to the surface. Our simmering stew of three distinct human cultures. Our landscapes. Our light."

Lawrence W. Cheek,
Arizona

A collecter's cornucopia: the rug room at J.L. Hubbell Trading Post, Ganado
PETER NOEBELS

Handmade clay pots standing sentry outside the Paloma Boutique in Tubac   DAVID W. LAZAROFF

The scarred hills surrounding Bisbee have yielded copper, silver, and gold   TOM TILL

The town of Jerome clings to the side of Mingus Mountain   LES MANEVITZ

A tourist's mecca, the town of Sedona sits just below the spectacular Mogollon Rim   BUDDY MAYS/TRAVEL STOCK

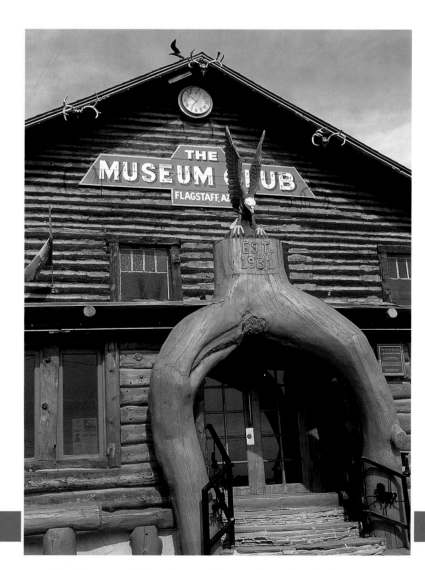

The Museum Club, a Flagstaff landmark on historic Route 66
SUSAN KAYE/TRAVEL STOCK

A sure sign that fall is on its way, the chile harvest is one of the most anticipated events of the year throughout the southwest   D. CAVAGNARO

> *At this very moment scientists are studying the X-quality that makes us eat chiles. Why do we want our mouths to burn? Is there too little excitement in otherwise predictable and ordered lives? . . . We know one thing for sure. Chiles are unpredictable, capricious devils.*

Jacqueline Higuera McMahan,
Red & Green Chile Book

47

Roasting green chiles at the Tucson Chile Festival
D. CAVAGNARO

Mariachis play the music of Mexico and stir the blood of many an Arizonan in Old Tucson   FRANK OBERLE

66 To that composite American identity of the future, Spanish character will supply some of the most needed parts. No stock shows a grander historic retrospect— grander in religiousness and loyalty, or for patriotism, courage, decorum, gravity and honor. 99

Walt Whitman,
*The Complete Prose Works
of Walt Whitman*

Traditional dancers in a rainbow of colors entertain at Tumacacori's December Fiesta
KERRICK JAMES

The music caresses the ears, the colors dazzle the eyes, the sky touches the soul   KERRICK JAMES

The former commissary at Fort Lowell RANDY A. PRENTICE

Brightly colored adobe in Tucson's Barrio Historico District KERRICK JAMES

Art deco architecture dominates Mercado Plaza in downtown Phoenix   RANDY A. PRENTICE

A very livable city: ducks navigating the lake at Phoenix's Encanto Park   RANDY A. PRENTICE

"As the mythical phoenix rose reborn from its ashes, so shall a great civilization rise here on the ashes of a past civilization. I name thee Phoenix!"

Darrel Duppa,
one of the first residents of Phoenix

New government building, downtown Phoenix   MIKE PADIAN

Downtown Tucson illuminated by sources man-made and heaven-sent   PETER NOEBELS

A rainbow arcs over Tucson's Pima County courthouse
RANDY A. PRENTICE

❝ *The City of Tucson sprawls beneath the sun in the Santa Cruz valley at the base of the Santa Catalina mountains. . . . Spaciousness and color lend distinctiveness to the physical setting. Low foothills ring the city and jagged peaks float in the distance. At every hour of the day they appear to change color as brown turns to lavender and then to deep blue at twilight. Amid the muted neutral colors of the desert the green palo verde, greasewood, and saguaro appear.* ❞

Arizona Memories

A line of saguaro cactus standing at attention as daylight fades   JACK W. DYKINGA

In any land what is there more glorious than sunlight! Even here in the desert, where it falls fierce and hot as a rain of meteors, it is the one supreme beauty to which all things pay allegiance.

John C. Van Dyke,
The Desert

Harris' hawk at Saguaro National Park
C. ALLAN MORGAN

Hedgehog cactus, brittlebush, teddybear cholla, saguaro, and palo verde at Organ Pipe Cactus National Monument
TOM DANIELSEN

Yellow blooms of the brittlebush backed up by organ pipe cactus and wispy clouds in an Arizona-blue sky   TOM DANIELSEN

The cheery blooms of a saguaro cactus greet the dawn at Saguaro National Park   JACK W. DYKINGA

Mexican gold poppies overgrowing a cholla cactus skeleton, Organ Pipe Cactus National Monument   WILLARD CLAY

Blossoms of the yellow barrel cactus   RANDY A. PRENTICE

Of all the desert perennials, I reserve my greatest admiration for the many members of the cactus family. Native to the Americas, they have diversified into more than a thousand species and have developed functionally into shapes so distinctive that the mind can never forget them. . . . They bloom with an extravagance of color, and during their time of flowering the desert wears them like gems.

Rowe Findley,
Great American Deserts

Ponderosa pines growing in a seemingly inhospitable environment, the cinder-covered Bonito lava flow, Sunset Crater Volcano National Monument   DAVID W. LAZAROFF

" If it is good to make occasionally what the religious call a "retreat," there is no better place than the desert to make it. Here if anywhere the most familiar realities recede and others come into the foreground of the mind. "

Joseph Wood Krutch,
The Voice of the Desert

Duck Rock perches precariously at Chiricahua National Monument   LES MANEVITZ

61

The Mustang Mountains and a blue September sky provide a backdrop for a stand of agave near Sonoita RANDY A. PRENTICE

The Kayenta Anasazi cliff dwelling called Keet Seel, in Navajo National Monument, consists of more than 150 rooms   TOM DANIELSEN

A ghostly pictograph in Monument Valley
PETER MARBACH/BORLAND STOCK

63

The Anasazi inhabited these cliff dwellings at Betatakin, which means "ledge house" in Navajo, more than 600 years ago   TOM DANIELSEN

"You cannot travel very long through Navajoland without stubbing your toe on the Anasazi. You can feel these things the children speak of, for the wind carries voices: Every conversation, every sigh uttered by the "long-time-ago people" circulates above you. Perhaps that's why the clouds move so quickly in the Southwest."

Terry Tempest Williams,
Pieces of White Shell

Indian sandals on display at the Museum of Northern Arizona, Flagstaff
KERRICK JAMES

As many as 125 people inhabited Betatakin, constructed in a natural sandstone amphitheater on the present-day Navajo National Monument
TOM DANIELSEN

Square House ruin, tucked away amid the fantastic rock formations in Monument Valley Navajo Tribal Park   TOM TILL

" The Navajo's concept of religion is so total that it can be said that there is no such thing as religion in Navajo culture because everything is religious. Everything a Navajo knows—his shelter, his fields, his livestock, the sky above him and the ground upon which he walks—is holy. "

Raymond Friday Locke,
The Book of the Navajo

A Navajo woman working wool in Monument Valley   ANN CECIL

The desert presents its own unique colors and shapes: Indian paintbrush and Navajo sandstone in the Paria Canyon Wilderness   JEFF FOOTT

> *In this land of distance and elusive horizons live the Navajos, whose love of their land is a religion. They are inured to the vagaries of the elements. They accept the wind, the Sun, the lack of rain, all the tempestuous quirks of time and weather—with stoic resignation, for all such things are their gods' will.*
>
> *They find their land good. It was good when they moved into it hundreds of years ago. It is good today. . . .*

Raymond Carlson,
Arizona's Scenic Seasons

Working sheep dogs, Monument Valley ANN CECIL

Sheep in the Monument Valley kicking up dust as they descend from their high grazing pastures   KATHLEEN NORRIS COOK

Riparian habitat along Aravaipa Creek near Hellhole Canyon RANDY A. PRENTICE

A fallen cottonwood provides a natural bridge across the clear waters of Sabino Creek in the Santa Catalina Mountains
DAVID W. LAZAROFF

In the1960s the London Bridge, which once spanned the Thames, was disassembled, shipped brick by brick to America, and reconstructed over an inlet of the Colorado River in Lake Havasu City RANDY A. PRENTICE

Jet skier on the Colorado BUDDY MAYS/TRAVEL STOCK

Anglers testing their skill on Saguaro Lake in the three-million-acre Tonto National Forest   TOM DANIELSEN

Successful angler at Tapeats Creek
CHARLIE BORLAND/BORLAND STOCK PHOTO

An evening sky is mirrored in the still waters of Crescent Lake in the White Mountains JACK W. DYKINGA

Mallard drake ERWIN AND PEGGY BAUER

Bullfrog SHERM SPOLESTRA

Sunflowers blooming at sunset, appropriately, below Sunset Crater RANDY A. PRENTICE

Yellow grosbeak ERWIN AND PEGGY BAUER

Tiger swallowtail butterfly BUDDY MAYS/TRAVEL STOCK

Symbols of the wild places in America, elk can be found in many of the mountainous areas of Arizona   DONALD M. JONES

Arizona can be cool, wet, and green: mountain hollyhock and sneezeweed blooming along the West Fork of the Little Colorado River
LARRY ULRICH

A pair of raccoon kits   SHERM SPOLESTRA

Silk-like, Havasu Creek slides over a ridge amid box elder and monkeyflower   LARRY ULRICH

Just one of the scenic wonders of the Grand Canyon, Havasu Falls spills into a blue-green pool   JAMES RANDKLEV

A stand of brittlebush giving off a golden glow at sunset in the Organ Pipe Cactus National Monument   WILLARD CLAY

66 *The real spirit of this desert world is in the sun-baked ground and in the strange plants and creatures that hail from it. The mystery may be too large and simple for any of us to ever fully appreciate, especially in the Mojave, where Nature plays her cards close to the vest, like the gambler she is.* 99

Larry Stevens,
Arizona: The Land and the People

Wildflowers bring beauty to the dry, cracked floodplains of the
Tohono O'Odham Indian Reservation   JACK W. DYKINGA

Not-so-cuddly teddybear cholla casting sunset shadows on the Kofa National Wildlife Refuge   JACK W. DYKINGA

A basketball-inspired mural adorns a Phoenix building across the street from America West Arena, home of the Phoenix Suns   JAMES RANDKLEV

Loyal fans flying high at the Thunderbird Balloon Fiesta in Glendale
KERRICK JAMES

Taking advantage of the warm weather, major league baseball comes to Arizona every spring   KERRICK JAMES

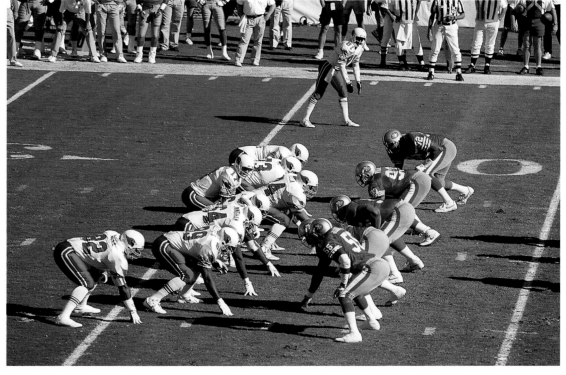

Arizona Cardinals taking on the San Francisco 49ers in Tempe   KERRICK JAMES

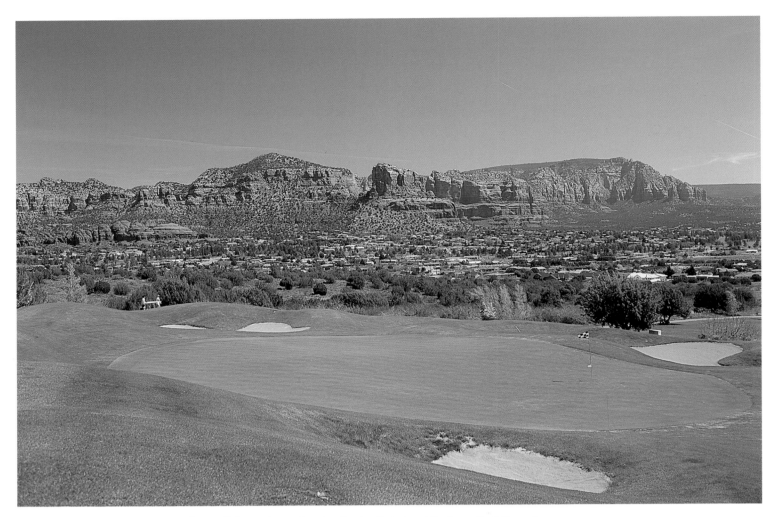

Green links under red rocks: the tenth hole at Sedona Golf Resort   ANN CECIL

" Turn off the sprinklers in summer and the golf courses will revert to desert. Cut the power and Arizonans will swelter. This paradise is ours by God's grace, man's ingenuity— and a few wires and pumps. "

Lawrence Clark Powell,
Arizona: A Bicentennial History

Camelback Mountain and palm trees adorning a golf course in Scottsdale   FRANK OBERLE

A swimming pool in every yard: bird's-eye view of part of Scottsdale   BUDDY MAYS/TRAVEL STOCK

Vacation homes at Twin Peaks Campground, Organ Pipe Cactus National Monument   ERIC WUNROW

A bull rider taking his licks at the Frontier Days Rodeo in Prescott   TOM BROWNOLD

Future cowpokes see how it's done   LONDIE G. PADELSKY

66 *Let the cowboy continue to gallop through the sagebrush and mesquite on a paint horse, popping his pistol and shouting 'yip-EEE'. . . . Let him wear a ten-gallon hat, a great neckerchief of silk, a shirt louder than a Rio Grande sunset, chaps of rawhide, shining boots, and musical spurs . . . . Let him have a strong chin and a pleasing drawl . . . . In emergencies let him always come through capable and modest. Keep him, keep him forever . . . .* 99

Oren Arnold,
Wonders of the West

Saddle bronc riding, an outgrowth of real cowboy work, is a uniquely American, uniquely Western pastime   TOM BROWNOLD

Rodeo is a game of speed, skill, courage, and tenacity   CHEYENNE ROUSE

Indian dancers preparing for a ceremonial dance in the colorful traditional clothes of America's original inhabitants   CHEYENNE ROUSE

" The dancing began! Skins, feathers, bones, shells, beads, claws, paint, and brightly colored fabrics. Shields, rattles, fans, sashes, breastplates, headdresses, moccasins, and jewelry. Each dancer a dream figure, proud and provocative. Together they walked slowly in a circle, chests high, chins lifted. I sat in awe, feeling as though I was being taken into an ancient trance. "

Terry Tempest Williams,
Pieces of White Shell

Let the dancing begin!   BUDDY MAYS/TRAVEL STOCK

Carrying on the tradition of his ancestors, a young Indian dances at Phoenix's Indian Village   BUDDY MAYS/TRAVEL STOCK

The next generation   PETER NOEBELS

Daylight fades and the sky turns a baby blue over the front peaks of the Kofa Mountains, Kofa National Wildlife Refuge   TERRY DONNELLY

"The desert of people is not my desert. I want open space. I want to see the animals and flowers of the desert, to hear the sounds of the dry, whistling winds, and the insects and the birds. The desert is largely a land of silence, but if you listen you can hear it."

Edmund C. Jaeger
Great American Deserts

91

Javelina SHERM SPOLESTRA

The heavily striated sandstone of Courthouse Butte near Sedona is a record of the past, each layer a clue to events unwitnessed by human eyes   RANDY A. PRENTICE

Quintessential Arizona: saguaro and organ pipe cactus in the Ajo Mountains at Alamo Wash, Organ Pipe Cactus National Monument
LARRY ULRICH

Nature's art: swirling sandstone patterns on the Colorado Plateau   LAURENCE PARENT

The frosted sand dunes of Monument Valley Navajo Tribal Park are etched by the natural forces of wind, sun, and rain   KATHLEEN NORRIS COOK

Snow graces the precise patterns of crosshatch sandstone strata in the Vermilion Cliffs Wilderness   JACK W. DYKINGA

An impossible-looking formation of sandstone flakes in the Vermilion Cliffs Wilderness   JACK W. DYKINGA

" The canyon walls rose straight up on either side of us, ranging from sunset orange to deep rust, mottled with purple. The sandstone had been carved by ice ages and polished by desert eons of sandpaper winds. The place did not so much inspire religion as it seemed to be religion itself. "

Barbara Kingsolver,
Animal Dreams

An illuminated wall in Slot Canyon, Navajo Reservation   LAURENCE PARENT

Smoke-like, cirrus clouds seem to be rising from behind a weathered butte in Monument Valley ERIC WUNROW

Morning fog shrouds jagged formations of the Santa Catalina Mountains above a hill of saguaro cacti RANDY A. PRENTICE

" The sun came out even before the hail stopped . . . . In a few minutes it was hot. I had on a big red pullover sweater and was starting to sweat. Arizona didn't do anything halfway. If Arizona was a movie you wouldn't believe it. You'd say it was too corny for words. "

Barbara Kingsolver,
The Bean Trees

A roadrunner speeding along the floor of the Sonoran Desert JEFF FOOTT

The moon rising behind a massive stone monolith and an impossibly tall century plant   TERRY DONNELLY

Blooming aloe adds crimson to the desert palette at Boyce Thompson Southwestern Arboretum near Superior   TOM TILL

Mourning dove on staghorn cholla   JAMES RANDKLEV

Cane cholla and beargrass   JACK W. DYKINGA

A bouquet of desert flora: chain fruit cholla, brittlebush, and red owl clover backed by the Puerto Blanco Mountains in Organ Pipe Cactus National Monument   JACK W. DYKINGA

Crested saguaro cactus   PETER NOEBELS

" Life in the desert is a wondrous, miraculous thing, but, perhaps, most wondrous and miraculous of all is the transformation of drab desert land into a veritable flower garden when rains come in winter and early spring. It doesn't happen every year, but when it does, it's worth waiting and watching for. "

Raymond Carlson,
Arizona's Scenic Seasons

Desert bighorn sheep, many of them wearing ear tags and radio collars for research, can be found in the mountain cliffs of Arizona BOB MILES

" . . . The desert, the dry and sun-lashed desert, is a good school
in which to observe the cleverness and the infinite variety of techniques
of survival under pitiless opposition. Life could not change the sun
or water the desert, so it changed itself. "

John Steinbeck,
Travels with Charley

Gila monster C. ALLAN MORGAN

Endangered desert tortoise ERWIN AND PEGGY BAUER

Burrowing owl GERRY ELLIS

Regal horned lizard C. ALLAN MORGAN

Jackrabbit SHERM SPOLESTRA

Fringe-toed lizard JEFF FOOTT

A setting sun seems to set fire to the grasslands and divides twin oak trees in the Coronado National Forest   JACK W. DYKINGA

A cool, welcoming scene in Cave Creek Canyon in the Chiricahua Mountains   RANDY A. PRENTICE

Higher than Niagara Falls, the Grand Falls on the Little Colorado River create a noisy, rushing cascade   LAURENCE PARENT

" *Nature might have made Sphinxes in her spare time*
Or Mona Lisas with her left hand,
Blindfolded.

Instead she gave the grain of sand,
The polished river stone,
The Grand Canyon. "

Terry and Renny Russell,
On the Loose

The majestic Grand Canyon from Toroweap: the Colorado River is 3,000 feet below   TOM DANIELSEN

A year-round native of Grand Canyon National Park, a mule deer munches on aspen leaves   JEFF FOOTT

A string of horses and their colts trotting along historic Route 66   LONDIE G. PADELSKY

❝ I noticed immediately a more bracing quality in the air; a clearer, bluer sky, a more buoyant note in the song of the birds; a snap and sparkle in the air that only Arizona air has, and I said to myself, without reference to a map, that we were now HOME. ❞

Former Senator Barry Goldwater

Wildflowers flourishing under a typical southwestern sky on the North Rim of the Grand Canyon at Cape Final   RANDY A. PRENTICE

Summer tanager   JEFF FOOTT

Black-headed grosbeak   CURT GIVEN

Scrub jay   CURT GIVEN

❝Birds color Navajoland like a living rainbow. According to the Dineh, in fact, rainbows get their colors from being lined with feathers. So often, I have sat on the desert with voluminous clouds encircling me and watched an arched prism with wings span the basin.❞

Terry Tempest Williams,
Pieces of White Shell

The floor and the ceiling of the earth: grasslands of the Navajo Indian Reservation and the endless Arizona sky   LAURENCE PARENT

❝ *Elsewhere the sky is the roof of the world; but here the earth was the floor of the sky. The landscape one longed for when one was far away, the thing all about one, the world one actually lived in, was the sky, the sky!* ❞

Willa Cather
Death Comes to the Archbishop

Sunrise reflected in the still waters of a desert oasis on the Cabeza Prieta National Wildlife Refuge   WILLARD CLAY

A stand of century plants on the grasslands near Sonoita is silhouetted against illuminated thunderheads at dusk   RANDY A. PRENTICE

Rising from the desert like the bow of a great ship, Weavers Needle, a weathered volcanic plug, reaches to 4,553 feet   TOM DANIELSEN

A bright moon rises over balanced and broken petrified logs in the Blue Mesa area   JACK W. DYKINGA

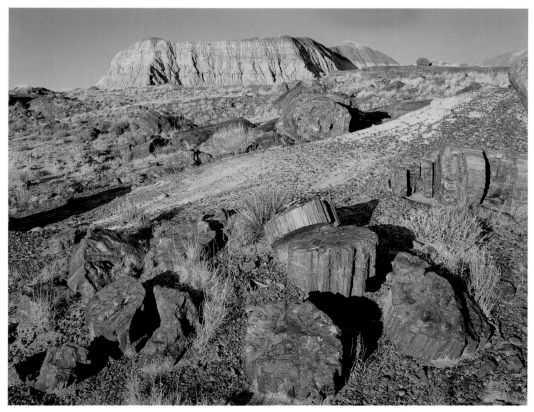

Scattered pieces of petrified logs, formed when they were buried in volcanic ash, decorating the floor of Petrified Forest National Park   TOM DANIELSEN

A pack rat's tracks lead the way to the Yei Bichai Dancers and Totem Pole formations on the Navajo Reservation   JACK W. DYKINGA

" I prefer the absences and the big empties, where the wind ricochets from sand grain to mountain. I prefer the crystalline dryness and an unadulterated sky strewn from horizon to horizon with stars. I prefer the raw edges and the unfinished hems of the desert landscape. "

Ann Zwinger,
The Mysterious Lands

The coyote, a desert survivor   JEFF FOOTT

A wind-blown tumbleweed leaves circular tracks on the desert floor in front of the Totem Pole and Yei Bichai Dancers formations in Monument Valley   JACK W. DYKINGA

they made it possible

Arizona on My Mind would have been impossible to produce without the keen eyes and technical skills of more than forty professional photographers. These men and women submitted their finest images, and the result shows in this stunning collection of photos. What does not show is the work it took to get these images—the early mornings to capture the sunrise, the long climbs through rugged terrain, the endless hours of waiting for the perfect light, the hundreds of shots that didn't turn out quite right, and the high level of technical skills that were acquired through years of experience and study. To all the photographers who contributed to *Arizona on My Mind*, we say thanks. We appreciate their art and their hard work.

The Globe Pequot Press

Photographers in *Arizona on My Mind*

Glen Allison

Erwin & Peggy Bauer

David Benner

Charlie Borland

Tom Brownold

David Cavagnaro

Ann Cecil

Willard Clay

Kathleen Norris Cook

Tom Danielsen

Terry Donnelly

Jack Dykinga

Gerry Ellis

Russ Finley

Jeff Foott

Mark Gibson

Curt Given

Kerrick James

Donald M. Jones

Susan Kaye

David W. Lazaroff

Les Manevitz

Peter Marbach

Buddy Mays

C. Allan Morgan

Peter Noebels

Frank Oberle

Londie G. Padelsky

Mike Padian

Laurence Parent

Randy A. Prentice

James Randklev

Randall K. Roberts

Cheyenne Rouse

Scott T. Smith

Sherm Spoelstra

Tom Till

Larry Ulrich

Eric Wunrow

Borland Stock Photo

F-Stock Inc.

Travel Stock

Library of Congress Number: 94-070153

ISBN 1-56044-496-7

Manufactured in Korea
First Edition/Eightth Printing

www.globe-pequot.com

Title page :
Painted Desert, Petrified Forest National Park
RUSS FINLEY/BORLAND STOCK PHOTO

End papers:
Saquaro cacti JACK DYKINGA

118

acknowledgments

The publisher gratefully acknowledges the following sources:

Page 1 from *Early Yuma. A Graphic History of Life in the American Nile*, Rosalie Crow and Sidney B. Brinckerhoff, eds. Copyright 1976 by Yuma County Historical Society. Published by Northland Press, Flagstaff, Arizona.

Page 3 from *The Grand Canyon: Early Impressions*, Paul Schullery, ed. Copyright 1981 by Paul Schullery. Published by Colorado Associated University Press, Boulder, Colorado.

Page 11 from *What Kinda Cactus Izzat?* Copyright 1941 by Reg Manning. Published by J. J. Augustin, New York.

Page 15 from *Arizona in Color* by Carlos H. Elmer. Copyright 1973 by Hastings House.

Pages 19, 37, 68, 101 from *Arizona's Scenic Seasons* by Raymond Carlson. Copyright 1984 by the Arizona Department of Transportation, Phoenix, Arizona.

Page 22 from *The Exploration of the Colorado River and Its Canyons*, by John Wesley Powell. Copyright 1961 by Dover Publications, New York.

Page 27 from *Blue Highways* by William Least Heat Moon. Copyright 1984 by William Least Heat Moon. Published by Ballantine, New York.

Pages 31, 59, 91 from *Great American Deserts* by Rowe Findley. Copyright 1972 by National Geographic Society, Washington, D.C.

Pages 33, 53 from *Arizona Memories*, Anne Hodges Morgan and Rennard Strickland, eds. Copyright 1984 by Arizona Board of Regents. Published by The University of Arizona Press, Tucson, Arizona.

Page 39 from *Tucson: The Life and Times of an American City*, by C. L. Sonnichsen. Copyright 1982 by C. L. Sonnichsen. Published by University of Oklahoma Press, Norman, Oklahoma.

Page 42 from *Arizona* by Lawrence W. Cheek. Copyright 1991 by Fodor's Travel Publications Inc. Published by Compass American Guides, Oakland, California.

Page 47 from *Red & Green Chile Book* by Jacqueline Higuera McMahan. Copyright 1987 by Jacqueline Higuera McMahan. Published by The Olive Press, Lake Hughes, California.

Page 48 from *The Complete Prose Works of Walt Whitman* by Walt Whitman. Copyright 1902, New York.

Pages 54, 84 from *Arizona: A Bicentennial History by Lawrence Clark Powell*. Copyright 1976 by W.W. Norton & Co. and the American Association for State and Local History.

Page 55 from *The Desert*, by John C. Van Dyke. Copyright 1987 by Peregrine Smith Books, Salt Lake City, Utah.

Page 60 from *The Voice of the Desert* by Joseph Wood Krutch. Copyright 1955 by Joseph Wood Krutch. Published by Morrow, New York.

Pages 63, 64, 88, 111 from *Pieces of White Shell: A Journey to Navajoland* by Terry Tempest Williams. Copyright 1983 by Terry Tempest Williams. Published by Charles Scribner's Sons, New York.

Page 66 from *The Book of the Navajo* by Raymond Friday Locke. Copyright 1976, 1979, 1986, 1989, 1992 by Raymond Friday Locke. Published by Mankind, Los Angeles.

Page 80 from *Arizona: The Land and the People*, Tom Miller, ed. Copyright 1986 by The University of Arizona Press, Tucson.

Page 86 from *Wonders of the West* by Oren Arnold. Copyright 1936 by Oren Arnold. Published by B. Upshaw & Co., Dallas.

Page 96 from *Animal Dreams* by Barbara Kingsolver. Copyright 1991 by Barbara Kingsolver. Published by HarperPerennials, New York.

Page 98 from *The Bean Trees* by Barbara Kingsolver. Copyright 1988 by Barbara Kingsolver. Published by HarperPerennials, New York.

Page 102 from *Travels with Charley* by John Steinbeck. Copyright 1962 by John Steinbeck. Published by Viking, New York.

Page 106 from *On the Loose* by Terry and Renny Russell. Copyright 1967 by Sierra Club, San Francisco.

Page 109 from *Call of the Colorado* by Roy Webb. Copyright 1994 by Roy Webb. Published by University of Idaho Press, Moscow, Idaho.

Page 112 from *Death Comes to the Archbishop* by Willa Cather. Copyright 1926, 1927, 1929 by Willa Cather. Published by Alfred A. Knopf, New York.

Page 116 from *The Mysterious Lands* by Anne Zwinger. Copyright 1990 by Anne Zwinger. Published by Plume Books, New York.

Reveling in the glow of another glorious Arizona outdoor adventure CHEYENNE ROUSE

" In beauty it is begun
In beauty it is finished
Go in beauty "

Navajo blessing